CONTENTS

ARRANGING FRESH & SILK FLOWERS

Silk flowers is the generic name for several styles of silk, polyester and paper flowers. There are freeze-dried silk flowers that look like dried flowers yet have the durability of fabric. There are beautiful, subtle shades of paper and vinyl flowers that have a sturdy appearance and velvety soft petals, that look and feel similar to fresh blooms. Prices for silk flowers vary from 49 cents to 50 dollars for a single rose...something for everyone! Many brands of 'ozone friendly' sprays to clean silk and dried flowers have made it possible to recycle arrangements for years.

HELPFUL HINTS FOR FRESH FLOWERS

1. Clean! Clean! Clean! Scour containers with a plastic pot cleaner, brush or sponge and put a few drops of chlorine bleach in the rinse water to cleanse the container of bacteria from previous arrangements before adding water for flowers. Debris and bacteria from previous arrangements will cause flowers to spoil quickly.

2. Remove all leaves and foliage below water line. Submerged leaves spoil the water, decay quickly, have an acrid odor and distract from the design.

3. Use high quality water...distilled, reverse osmosis or dionized water.

4. Cut stems under water. This keeps air in the stem to a minimum and speeds water to the head of the flower.

5. Cut ends of stems on a slant and crush the ends of thick stems before placing in arrangement to insure maximum water absorption.

6. Use preservatives. They enhance the color and lasting ability of your arrangement.

7. Cut foam to fit inside of container leaving a well around sides for water to be drawn through foam. Allow foam to reach 1" above the rim of the vase so you can insert flowers to glide sideways or gracefully around the top. Hide the foam with flowers or moss.

STORING FLOWERS FOR FUTURE USE

Remove all foliage from lower stems and cut ends with a sharp knife or scissors (underwater). Quickly lay flowers with heads together on piece of foil and wrap securely. Place in a clean container with enough cold water to cover the bottom 2" of stems. Store in a cold room or a cool, airy, place.

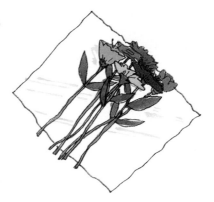 

HELPFUL HINTS FOR SILK FLOWERS

1. Anchor non-porous, plastic foam with hot melt glue, glue gun, or plastic frog held in place with clay (or just stuff the container with absorbent oasis foam.

2. Camoflage mechanics with moss.

3. Gently bend flowers and leaves into soft, natural curves before inserting flowers into foam.

4. If the stems swivel, slit the tape and separate the wires into a fork before pushing the stem into the foam. You can also twist another wire around the base of the stem to form an extra 'leg'.

5. Silk bushes, pre-formed silk bouquets and greenery can be cut into several stems for many arrangements. Lengthen stems by wiring (see wiring techniques).

6. Dip stems in pan glue, white glue or hot glue before inserting them in the foam for more permanent designs.

7. Insert leaves into foam to fill out the design before adding the flowers.

Helpful Hints for Fresh and Silks

1. Position a container with three legs to show one leg directly in front.

2. Rotate the stems so the flowers face different directions.

3. Insert flowers of the same length at different angles.

4. Allow breathing space between flowers to prevent a crowded look.

5. Use flowers in different stages of development from bud to full bloom.

6. When using tall containers, oasis foam and scraps of plastic foam can be salvaged, cut into small pieces and stuffed inside the container to hold flowers in place.

7. Fillers such as sand, Kitty Litter or even bird gravel can be used to raise the floor of the container . If the container tends to topple over you can also add marbles to the bottom for ballast.

Cleaning silks

They can be sloshed around in warm water and a mild detergent in the bath tub or sink. They can be damp dusted. There are aerosol sprays for cleaning silks. Test a small area first. Paper flowers can only be dusted with a feather duster or blown with a hairdryer on a low setting. Manipulate the petals and leaves so they have a natural look and they aren't crushed or bent. Paper flowers can be re-shaped by lightly steaming and slightly pulling and rolling the flower petals in the desired direction.

Centerpieces

When arranging flowers for a centerpiece, make it low so it doesn't interfere with conversation. The container should be in character with the settings. Wicker looks better with pottery and plastic, and silver and crystal look better with china. If the dishes are colorful, select most of the arranging material in the hue that appears in the smallest quantity in the china.

Having control over the length, strength and flexibility of a stem is a great advantage in flower arranging. When a flower stem has two or more blossoms, you can cut off the blooms and give each flower a new stem. These techniques can be used on fresh, silk or dried flowers.

BASIC TECHNIQUE FOR TAPING A WIRED STEM

1. Wrap a piece of floral tape around the top of the wire and press in place.

2. Twirl the stem while stretching and pulling the tape in a downward angle. The tape should be tightly wrapped around the wire without buckles or gaps along the stem.

PIERCE METHOD

For flowers with a thick calyx beneath the flower head, such as roses and carnations:

1. Trim stem to 1/2 to 1 inch, Push one end of a wire horizontally through the calyx using half the length of the wire.

2. Bend both ends down parallel with the stem and tape, starting just above the pierce.

Note: A second wire may be inserted through the flower so that the two wires are criss crossed for heavy flowers.

HOOK METHOD

1. Cut flower stem to about 1 inch long. Push a wire along or through the stem until the wire comes through the center of the flower to a height of about 1 1/2".

2. Form a 1/2 to 3/4" hook and pull the wire back down through the flower. The end of the hook should emerge back through the base of the flower. Tape the stem.

INSERTION METHOD

1. If flower head is firmly attached to stem, using 6 to 9 inch wire, cut the flower stem to 1 inch long and push the wire inside the stem, up into the flower head until it is firm.

2. Tape stem and wire tightly.

CLUTCH METHOD

Any flowers can be wired in this manner, but it is expecially good for small clusters of flowers.

1. Cut the flower stems to 1 1/2" long and wrap a light wire around the cluster tightly to create the appearance of a small bouquet.

2. Bend the two wire ends parallel to the stem and tape.

FLOWER SUPPORTS

This method adds strength and flexibility to the stem allowing the flower to be bent.

1. Insert a full-length wire vertically into the base of the calyx.

2. Loosely wrap the wire around the full length of the stem in a spiral. Tape the stem to cover the wire.

WIRELESS TAPING

1. To create free flowing pieces with small flowers for a corsage or hairpiece, cut the stem to 1" long.

2. Wrap a piece of floral tape around the top of the stem and twirl the flower in one hand while twisting the tape lightly around itself until it's as long as you want it. (If you need more support, tape it again.)

They transcend their useful purpose and become an artistic component of the over-all design, an integral part of it. The only practical requirement for containers, forms and bases is that they be sturdy enough to balance the weight and breadth of the selected arrangement material.

Forms

Abstract forms, like interesting driftwood or graceful branches, are distinguished by size, color and texture; the whole makes a pattern in space. Forms can be used with or without containers.

Flowering trees and shrubs such as: dogwood, tree lilac, star magnolia, pear and quince have well-shaped, bare branches for arrangements. Many can be found along the road after a storm or during tree removals.

Wood forms found inland, usually need considerable grooming. Partially decayed and covered with dirt they require strong hosing, scraping with a stiff wire brush and chisel, or soaking and scrubbing with soap and water. Sanding the surface improves the texture. Varnish stain or wax enhances grain and color.

Carved by wind, water and rock, driftwood may emerge as a completed work of art. Clean and shining, it needs no refinement. Shapes may be altered by removing some of the portions and relocating them to improve the height or

Driftwood form

balance. Segments may be added to increase size, or when combining two or more pieces, to produce a more complex form.

Although the finish seldom needs retouching, the surface highlights may be enhanced by shading with pastel chalk, which can be washed off if you don't like the effect. A light application of clear plastic spray will protect the wood and make it easier to clean.

As sculptural characteristics become visible, the form can be studied from all sides to determine possible reshaping and mounting. If sections need to be removed and relocated, epoxy glue is a good bonding agent. Metal rods or sections of wire coat hangers can also join segments. Inserted into holes drilled into the wood and properly fitted, segments can be joined without gluing.

Containers

Start collecting containers: a shallow bowl, cylinder, compote, goblet, trough shape, oval, baskets, urn...look for the unusual. They don't have to be watertight. Choices can range from a tiny shell for a miniature arrangement to a large stone urn for a large room or impressive building.

Containers need to be suitable for the setting and complement the atmosphere of the room. Baskets blend especially well with either vibrant or muted shades of flowers and are well suited to informal settings and country style furnishings.

Brass, copper, silver and pewter can be beautiful complements to arrangements and come in a variety of sizes, shapes and functions. Wrought ironwork can also add a distinctive look to flowers and foliage.

Containers

Goblets, wine glasses, builders glass bricks, modern glass sculptures and a variety of glass vases are all attactive material for flower arrangements. The plumbing department of your local hardware store is a goldmine for interesting shapes and sizes. PVC pipe can be hot glued onto a wooden base and fashioned into unusual containers.

Old earthenware jars, ovenware, hand-thrown pottery, clay drainage pipes and ornate china also make interesting containers for flower arrangements.

Keep containers clean! Wash with detergent and rinse with bleach water. Unglazed pottery and ceramic vases will leak, so they can either be sealed with five coats of waterproof sealant, allowing each layer of sealer to dry thoroughly before applying the next one, or they can be fitted with a plastic liner. Plastic cups and glass cylinders also make good liners.

Lining Baskets

Baskets will hold foam and water if they are lined with heavy plastic.

1. Line the basket to the edge of the lip with heavy plastic.

2. Place foam in basket.

3. Loop a #24 wire through the weave at the lip of the basket and pull the wire over the foam. Secure the wire to the opposite side of the basket lip.

Lining Glass Containers

When making an arrangement using foam in a clear glass vase, you can hide the foam by lining the inside of the vase with silver mylar, a lightweight, polyester material.

Forms, Containers, & Bases

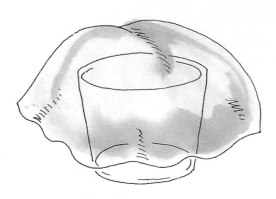

1. Cut a piece of mylar slightly larger than the container. If the mylar is large enough to cover the outside, it will fit the inside.

2. Place a soaked piece of floral foam into the mylar-lined vase.

3. Fill the container with water. Pull up gently on the excess mylar around the edge of the vase. Leave it as a ruffle or trim even with the edge of the container.

Bases

A base of slate or a cross-cut of wood can be used as a platform to work from and can also contribute to the shape and mood of the design. For a more formal arrangement the wood can be covered with velvet, and for a less formal style with a sturdy fabric such as burlap. Polished or unpolished wood, cork, blamboo, clear plastic sheets, blocks of plexiglass and polished marble are all excellent and versatile materials for bases.

The mainstay of any floral design is the device that holds it together. Anchors to support an arrangement must be firmly secured and inconspicuous. These are the mechanics used for both fresh and silk flowers. Dried flowers are light and don't require the anchoring that live or silk flowers need to hold them in place. A vase full of oasis foam is usually the only support a dried arrangement requires.

Florist Foam

There are many types of floral foam available. It comes in rounds, sticks or blocks of various styles and sizes. Each one has a specific purpose. It can easily be cut to the appropriate size with a knife or small saw.

Blocks of foam can be glued together to raise or widen them. Glue a piece of hard foam under a piece of absorbent foam when working with a combination of heavy branches and fine-stemmed fresh, silk or dried flowers.

When preparing foam for fresh flowers, immerse the floral foam slowly into a sink or pail of preservative treated water until all the air has been released. Insert a knife several times to allow pockets of air to bubble up. Make sure sinks and pails are free from soap or any chemical residue. Then place in container and add water.

The weight of the water soaked foam holds it in place for small arrangements. For larger ones, the wet foam can be anchored to a pin holder that has been glued to the bottom of the vase. The wet foam can also be secured by taping it in place.

Plastic foam is a coarse, non-porous foam. It's a good choice for working with large silk flowers. It can be cut to shape and wedged into a container or anchored to the bottom with clay, hot glue, or pan melt glue.

Desert foam is also coarse and non-porous and is easier to penetrate than plastic foam.

Sahara foam is a finer, non-porous foam which is generally used with fresh and dry materials, because it is easy to penetrate and will not break fragile stems.

Oasis foam is highly absorbent and used to maintain fresh plants. It can also be used as a filler for tall vases and when combining fresh and silk flowers. Absorbent foam, used for both silk or fresh flowers can be stuffed inside the container, leaving a space between the foam and the sides so water can be transferred through the block to the flowers.

Waterproof tape is a special tape used for securing foam. Double-sided tape florist tape can also be used.

Press the end of the tape to the side of a clean, dry container. If dirt or an oily residue prevents the tape from adhering to the container, clean the area with hand cleaner or nail polish remover. The tape will stick after the area dries.

Floral tape is available in a variety of colors. It sticks to itself and is used to wrap around wire flower stems on silks or to support delicate stems on fresh flowers (see Wiring Techniques).

Floral wire a green enameled wire that comes in different weights is used to extend stems or support flowers cut from original stems. The higher the gauge number the thinner the wire.

A plastic frog (or anchor pins) is a circle of plastic (which is adhered to the bottom of the container) with several upright prongs on which foam is impaled.

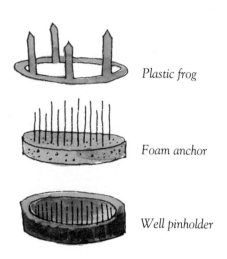

Plastic frog

Foam anchor

Well pinholder

A foam anchor has a heavy metal base with long widely-spaced pins similar in function to a plastic frog.

A well pinholder is a small container with vertical pins inside. Pinholders are helpful when combining fresh and fabric flowers, including natural and dried foliage with heavy stems. To support the wire stems of silk flowers, attach a piece of sahara foam over the pins.

Waterproof clay that is non-drying and reusable is used to anchor plastic frogs, well pinholders and foam anchors. (Make sure the surface is absolutely dry and free of dust or the clay won't stick to the container or anchor.)

Pan Melt Glue can secure dry foam in many containers. Melt the pellets of glue in an electric pan or regular pan on low heat on the stove. When glue is melted, but not hot, dip the four corners of the floral foam into the glue and place in container. (A glue gun can also be used to adhere foam or frogs in place.)

Candlecups are small, inexpensive containers designed to fit on candlesticks and can also be fitted into the necks of bottles. Comparable to a needle holder, a cupholder is a small receptacle and needle-holder welded together. Though shallow, a cupholder can accomodate a sizeable arrangement by placing a piece of foam well into the pins of the holder and securing the foam and candlecup to the candlestick or bottle with clay, florist tape or 22 gauge wire. They are available in various sizes and are made in chrome, brass, copper and white or colored plastic.

Hiding the Anchors

Reindeer moss soaked until it is soft and pliable can be placed over the foam before the flowers are inserted. Flora and fauna can be arranged near the rim of the container to conceal the supports. Spaghnum moss, the kind you find growing on the ground, rocks or at the base of trees, spanish moss, a string-like moss that grows on trees in the South or bulb fibre can also be used to disguise the mechanics. Greening pins, 'u' shaped or hairpin-like wire pins can be inserted through moss and dried material and into the floral foam to hold it in place.

Stones, driftwood or pebbles also make good camoflage. In modern, free-form arrangements the foam can be colored to match the container or base by spraying it lightly (outside) with water base, acrylic, aerosol paint.

GRIDS FOR HOLDING FLOWERS IN PLACE

Crumpled turkey wire

Oasis sticks

Lead crossbar sling

1" chicken wire basket

Scotch tape

1. Create a crisscross grid with clear tape.

2. Bend the edges of the chicken wire over and into the foam inside the vase. If you aren't using foam, bend the chicken wire to inside lip of vase and hold it in place with waterproof tape or 22 gauge wire.

3. Lead crossbar slings can be held in place with wire.

4. Crumpled turkey wire and pinholder provide a good grid for small stem flowers. Slip silks or fresh flowers in place through wire. It's a good method for combining fresh and silk flower arrangements.

5. Oasis foam also comes in sticks and can be easily stuffed into vases for supporting the arrangement and holding it in place. (You can also use scraps of foam the same way.)

LACING FERNS

Lacing ferns is a quick and easy technique. Cut 8 fern stems 2 inches shorter than the height of the vase.

1. Insert one stem in between the last and next to last frond at the bottom of the first fern.

2. Insert third fern in between the last and next to last frond on the second piece of fern.

3. The fourth fern is inserted in the same location of the third piece of fern.

4. Continue lacing the ferns inserting the fifth in the fourth and the sixth in the fifth and so on until all 8 ferns have formed a grid.

Sit the grid securely inside the lip of the container. (It is also possible to use a 4 leaf grid on some arrangements.)

Flowers, either fresh, dried or silk, have different characteristics that lend themselves to different functions in an arrangement.

Line flowers stand tall and have many blossoms close to the stem. They give a basic shape and direction to the arrangement. Line flowers are 'showy'. Gladiolas, snapdragons, delphinium and stock are examples of line flowers. In the illustration, two snapdragons are used to establish the structure of the design.

Filler florals have clusters of individual flowers on a single stem or flower head. Some fillers have multiple leaves and feathering blooms. They are transitional flowers and fill spaces between the line and focal flowers. Gypsophila, statice, pompoms and waxflowers are examples of filler florals. Gypsophilia is a popular filler around roses.

Focal flowers are single stem, compact florals that command the attention of the viewer and are placed close to the center of the arrangement slightly above and below the lip of the container. They add weight and volume to a design and are almost always round flowers like carnations, roses and asters. The illustrations show roses as an example.

COMMON NAMES
OF LINE, FOCAL & FILLER PLANTS & FLOWERS

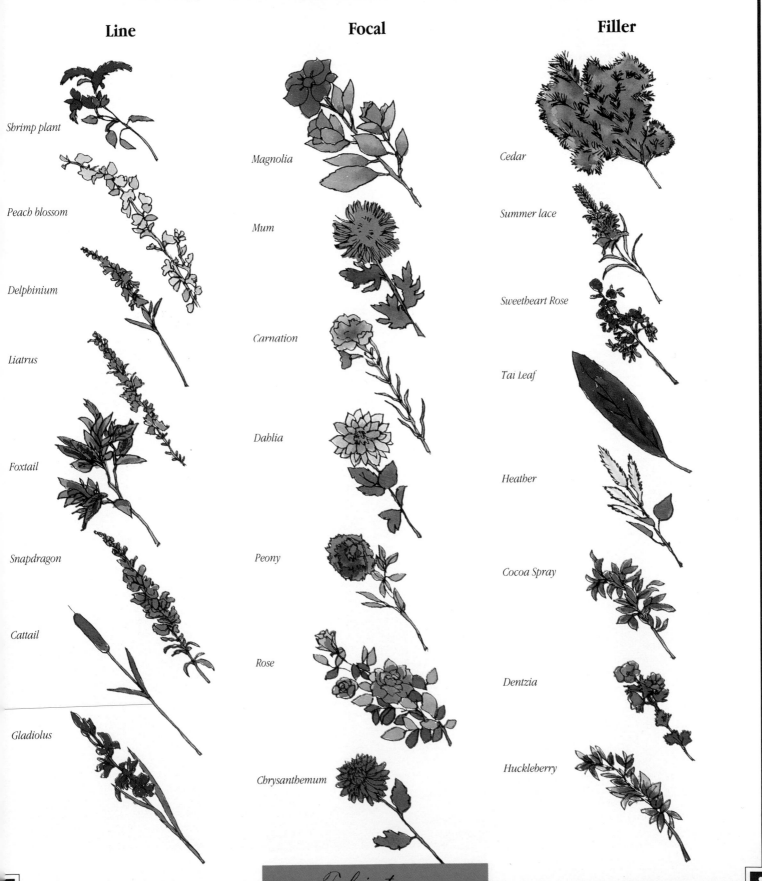

Line

Shrimp plant

Peach blossom

Delphinium

Liatrus

Foxtail

Snapdragon

Cattail

Gladiolus

Focal

Magnolia

Mum

Carnation

Dahlia

Peony

Rose

Chrysanthemum

Filler

Cedar

Summer lace

Sweetheart Rose

Tai Leaf

Heather

Cocoa Spray

Dentzia

Huckleberry

EIGHT BASIC DESIGNS

There are eight basic ways to structure a flower arrangement, but within each shape the use of scale, variation of emphasis, choice of colors, containers and textures provides the imagination with endless creative possibilities. Different cultures contribute a variety of styles.

Horizontal arrangements are often used for centerpieces, tables, window sills...anywhere a long arrangement is suitable. Wider horizontal arrangements suggest a natural growth pattern by using simple lines of flowers instead of a central axis.

1. Using a relatively shallow container, anchor foam and position sprays of line flowers to establish design.

2. Insert focal flowers in middle so they gently droop over lip of container on both sides, reaching up towards line material and extending on either side of middle leaving room for filler florals.

3. Fill in around focal area with flowers and foliage.

Vertical arrangements offer a continuous line of movement upward. Iris, arum lily, calla lilies, larkspur, eucalyptus or bird of paradise are often used. Tall, slender designs are excellent where space is limited.

1. Secure foam in a vase. (See section on Mechanics.) Cut tallest flower or leaf 3 or 4 times the height of the vase to set the height, balance and central axis of the arrangement.

2. Place all other flowers vertically within the diameter of the vase. Width lines are restricted, extending slightly to the right or left .

3. Fill in areas as needed with Filler florals and soften the container rim with leaves and sprays of light colored flowers.

Seventeen

Triangular arrangements are pleasing in traditional settings. The shape may be equally balanced on each side or asymmetrical with one point of the triangle extending further than the other. A variety of sizes, shapes, textures and kinds of flowers can be used. Stems radiate from a central area with paler and smaller flowers and leaves at the outer edges and deep colored or brighter blooms near the center. The larger arrangements are often used for altars, weddings and large parties. (Smaller triangle arrangements, used for special occasions and holidays, are usually equilateral with a central vertical axis. Sometimes one half of the arrangement mirrors the other.)

Since the flower stems and foliage, along with the wet foam (when using fresh flowers) can become quite heavy in this type of design, the foam should be fully packed to the bottom of the container.

3. Fill in with smaller flowers and foliage keeping within the triangular shape.

1. Determine vertical height and horizontal width with smallest flowers and leaves. Make height higher than width.

2. Position largest flowers in heart of arrangement and slightly lower to give weight and balance.

Nineteen

A Crescent is a segment of a circle that resembles a new moon. The curved line of this arrangement gives it a graceful look which is appealing to the eye. Flexible, wiry stems of silk flowers can be smoothed into curves with a gentle pressure of thumbs and forefingers, or they can be placed in hot water (110 degrees) for a few minutes to soften them enough to curve the stems, and then placed in cold water to 'set' the curve. (You can hold them under the faucet.)

3. Fill in around focal flowers with smaller flowers and foliage. Place wisps of filler floral that gracefully tapers off ends.

1. Secure foam in container. Determine length of crescent and insert curved line flowers or leaves to follow crescent form. Angle crescent to balance in container.

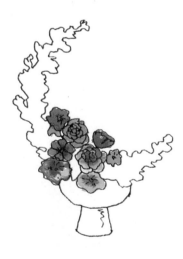

2. Insert focal flowers fairly low to achieve balance and depth.

Twenty one

Oval arrangements have a similar appearance from all sides. They can be constructed in a formal way with larger blooms centrally placed and smaller ones echoing around the edges. One of my favorites is a casual design that looks like a large handful of blooms grasped from a flower-filled field that settle into a generous container and spread out like a giant oak tree. But, it's never that simple. There is an art to making an arrangement look natural. Flowers arranged in an oval or round design last longer because they are closer to the water source. It's easier to arrange all sides by working on a lazy susan. If the vase isn't stable, tape it in place with floral tape so it doesn't topple over while you are arranging the flowers. Oval arrangements look great on the coffee table, as a room divider, or on a bedside table.

1. Determine height, then frame in outer edges of oval with light colored flowers and foliage.

2. Place largest, strongest or brightest flowers in focal area. Keep turning arrangement as you place flowers so design is pleasing from all sides.

3. Fill in around larger flowers and leaves and soften edges with smallest filler flora.

Twenty three

EIGHT BASIC DESIGNS

Minimal arrangements make use of space as a design element, and styling is done with an economy of materials. They present quiet, subtle and dramatic understatements. Arrangements can have groups of the same flowers to project a mood or atmosphere.

3. Fill in as needed.

1. Adhere foam to container. Anchor verticals to determine height and secure horizontals to give basic outline of arrangement.

2. Place focal flowers.

Twenty five

The lazy 'S' or 'Hogarth curve' was named for a painter called William Hogarth who loved flowers. He took two pieces of a circle and put them together to create a graceful line that looks like an 's'.

3. Cluster blossoms and foliage around central flowers maintaining the rhythm of the 's'.

1. Anchor foam securely. Bend wire stems of silk flowers (using thumbs and forefingers) into graceful curves. Insert in place so they balance.

2. Add focal flowers following lines of upper and lower curves.

Free Standing arrangements are similar to ovals in the universality of their shape and their circular design. But ovals have a gently rounded arc at the top, and free standing arrangements come to a definite point at the top like a Christmas tree. They include an abundance of flowers and can be placed in a wide variety of places.

3. Add filler flora to integrate design.

1. Fill shallow container with foam one inch over top. If arrangement is large, cover foam with chicken wire, bending edges back into foam and securing with floral tape (see Mechanics). Hide mechanics with moss secured with 'u' pins. If using silk flowers you won't need the chicken wire. If container is large, just fill with oasis foam (add ballast if needed). Define shape of design with line flowers and leaves.

2. Place focal flowers and leaves turning arrangement so all sides are even (a lazy susan is helpful).

Twenty nine

Color

When you think of colors emotions begin to stir because colors are associated with people, events, moods, music, warmth and coolness. When you begin to look more deeply into the nature and physics of color you develop the ability to select instead of react; you begin to use your free will instead of your conditional or psychological response. Learning more about color allows you to experiment with a greater range of possibilities within yourself and in your designs.

There are no 'wrong' colors or combinations of colors. Colors offer complete freedom of choice within the spectrum. Whatever is pleasing to you is right for you. If your choice is different from someone elses we are reminded to appreciate the differences. Within each of us is a natural desire for certain colors at certain times. We crave it like we long for the sun in the middle of winter. It comforts us on many levels.

Traditional Color Combinations

The color wheel divides colors into warm and cool colors. The warm colors are red, orange and yellow. Cool colors are green, blue and violet. Warm colors are more 'out going' they move to meet you; cool colors shy away. Warm colors require less light to be seen and cool colors come alive when they are in the spot light. The full intensity of a color is called a 'hue', a 'tint' is a hue lightened with white, a 'tone' is a hue mixed with gray and a 'shade' is a hue darkened with black.

Colors slip into the sphere of music because they can be harmonious, discordant, vibrant or muted. Monochromatic means 'one color'. Pink, rose, mauve and burgundy flowers in a design is an example of a monochromatic color harmony. It consists of tints and shades of a single color. The energy is subtle and soothing.

Analogous colors are next to each other on the color wheel. They create a rhythmic flow by including one primary color and at least one-fourth of the color wheel. Yellow, yellow-orange, orange and red-orange blend to create a popular color harmony for autumn arrangements.

Complementary colors are opposite one another on the color wheel. Violets and yellows, peaches and greens create a soft contrast and have an enlivening effect on each other. Complementary colors are good for spring arrangements.

A triad of colors consists of any three colors equally spaced that fall at the points of a triangle placed anywhere on the color wheel. Red, yellow, blue or orange, green and violet are combined to create an exciting, lively color harmony.

Use the color wheel to relate flower colors to your room colors and to combine flower colors within the arrangement itself. The largest areas in a room, the walls and floors, are usually color coordinated in tints and shades of complementary, analygous and monochromatic colors.

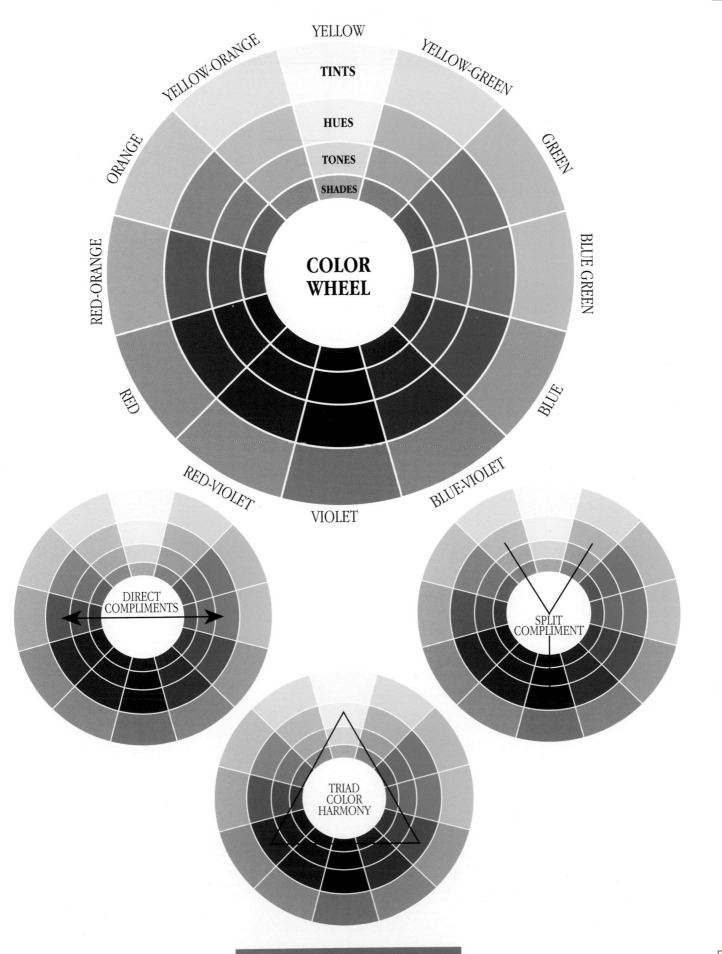

COLOR
WHEEL

YELLOW

YELLOW-ORANGE · YELLOW-GREEN

TINTS

ORANGE · GREEN

HUES

TONES

SHADES

RED-ORANGE · BLUE GREEN

RED · BLUE

RED-VIOLET · BLUE-VIOLET

VIOLET

DIRECT
COMPLIMENTS

SPLIT
COMPLIMENT

TRIAD
COLOR
HARMONY

SEASONAL ARRANGEMENTS
FALL

Flowers provide changing interest throughout the year. The change in seasons is often accompanied with a change in emotions. Artists use the universal mandala of Spring, Summer, Winter and Fall to express layers of feelings, cycles of change and the continuity of life. What better way to express our participation in the 'Grand Theme' than by celebrating each variation with flowers.

FALL FLORALS

Gladiolus, Snapdragons, Stock, Larkspur, Canterbury, Cattail, Delphinium, Wheat Spray, Heather Peonies, Chrysanthemum, Dahlia, Crown Aster, Rose, Petunia, Scabiosa Hybiscus, Camellia, Passion Flower, Anemony, Begonias, Debutante Rose, African Daisy, Snowball, Marigold, Spider Azalia, Wax Berry Foliage, Carnation, Pom pom, Clover, Star Aster, Mountain Daisy

SEASONAL ARRANGEMENTS
WINTER

Winter belongs to Camellias and Cymbidium orchids. Depending upon the climate zone many flowers, bulbs and shrubs thrive on the chill of shortened days and colder nights.

SEASONAL ARRANGEMENTS
SPRING

The fragrance of Spring can be as memorable as its appearance. Warm and humid days carry layers of aromas to delight our senses and arrest our perception.

SEASONAL ARRANGEMENTS
SUMMER

V ibrant marigolds and gloriosa daisies
chronicle the advent of summer at its zenith.
From sun to shade irrepressible flowers and
plants celebrate a time to dance with the season.

SUMMER FLORALS

Delphinium, Larkspur, Liatrus, Bells of Ireland, Gladiolas, Gladder, Chrysanthe-
mums, Scabiosa, Roses, Dahlias, Cholla, Pavillon, Peony Camellia, Passion
Flower, Fringe Aster, Princess Lace, Zinnia, Cosmos, African Daisy, Rhododen-
dron, Celosia, Calendula, Cosmos, Impatience, Lobelia, Mimulus, Petunias,
Sweet Williams, Four O'clocks, Phlox, Candytuft, Sunflowers, Amarylis,
Agapantha, Canna, Cyclamen, Verbena, Gazania, Jasmine, Periwinkle,
Heliotrope, Gardenias, Magnolias, Strawflowers, Wisteria, Statice

DRIED FLOWERS

Like silk and fresh flowers, preserved flowers and foliage have a charm of their own. Combining flowers from different seasons, they make lovely, unusual bouquets. When designed into patterns or pictures and framed or added to ribbons and hats they remind us of fragrant, warm, sunny days and special times in our life. There are many time-honored ways to preserve flowers and plants.

SIX DIFFERENT WAYS TO DRY FLOWERS

Pressing

Delicate flowers like pansies and violets can be placed between sheets of absorbent paper and inserted between the pages of an old telephone book. In two to three weeks, the weight of the book will press out the plant moisture which is absorbed by the paper. This technique is good for personalized greeting cards or stationery because the flowers and leaves dry flat.

Whole branches, ferns, bracken and spiky leaves can be dried this way. To dry foliage, arrange the material in a single layer on several pieces of newspaper, no overlapping. Cover with more newspaper and put the "parcel" under some pressure.

Air Drying

Sturdier flowers like bells of Ireland, roses, statice, gypsophylia, yarrow and larkspur dry well using the air-dry method. Strip off all the leaves as soon as possible. The leaves retain moisture and will slow down the drying process. Dry large flowers individually. Bunches should contain only one type of flower. Tie together in small bundles and hang upside down in a warm, place away from direct sunlight until dry. The flower heads of many of the straw flowers are too heavy for the dried stems to support. Cut and wire before hanging out to dry. The air-drying process usually takes 2 to 3 weeks.

Preserving

Miniature oak, maple and magnolia leaves, baby's breath and eucalyptus are frequently dried by mixing fhree parts water to one part glycerine. The stems of flowers or foliage are placed in the glycerine and water. As the glycerine is absorbed through the plant, it becomes 'embalmed' so that it is dried yet still supple. Material treated with glycerine lasts indefinitely and can be dusted or even wiped with a damp cloth without risk.

Water Drying

Strip off the leaves and place the flower stem in 2" of water in a warm, cozy place. The water is absorbed and evaporated as the flower dries. Hydrangeas, proteas, heathers and yarrow dry well this way.

Drying in Dessicants

Cut off the heads and cover them for a week with a blanket of silica gel or an equal mixture of borax and cornmeal. Zinnias, roses, larkspur, daffodils, dahlias, marigolds, carnations, camellias and pansies are suitable for dessication. Though this is the least predictable way to preserve blooms, the effects can be dazzling and life-like preserved flowers. Pick in perfect condition, on a dry day just before maturity. Flowers can be wired before drying.

The dessicant must be completely dry before you begin. Warm it in the oven for a half hour first. Put a layer of desiccant in the bottom of a plastic storage box. Carefully coat each flower head. Dry one type at a time. Pour desiccant over each flower separating the petals carefully with a toothpick as you pour. Shake container a little bit to settle the desiccant. Cover the flowers completely. Cover container with a tight fitting lid and store in a warm, cozy place.

Check in 4-5 days. If the flowers feel papery, they are ready to remove. If not, cover them carefully and check again in 2 days. If they are left for too long in silica gel they get brittle and dark. Borax and cornmeal doesn't alter the color as much. Brush off desiccant with a soft artist brush.

DRIED FLOWERS

Adding wire stems to dried flowers

1. Cut each flower head from the spray so that the stem is approximately 1 1/2" long.

1 1/2"

2. Using 20 gauge wire, cut wire to the desired length, allowing extra for bending and for the part of the stem to be inserted into the floral foam. Bend tip of wire with pliers to form a 'shepherd's hook'.

3. Hook wire around the calyx, where the flower head joins the stem, and squeeze tightly with needle-nose pliers.

4. Wrap green floral tape over wire from top to bottom.

Restoring silica gel

Silica gel has a strong absorbing property. It is ideal for drying flowers because the small granules easily penetrate even the most delicate flower heads. It is sold in garden shops, drugstores, craft shops and floral shops.

When dry, silica gel is blue, but the granules become a whitish-pink as they absorb moisture. You can tell when the silica granules have reached their saturation point by checking the color. Silica gel can be re-used for years by removing the moisture from the granules each time they become saturated.

To restore silica gel for re-use, preheat oven to 300 degrees. Sift through to remove as much left-over plant material as possible. Spread a single layer of silica gel evenly on the bottom of a shallow pan and place it uncovered in the oven. Stir every so often and watch for the return of the original blue color. Cool completely and store in a tight-fitting, covered container.

To restore silica gel on the stove, place a layer in an uncovered low, wide, non-teflon frying pan on medium heat. Stir from time to time until the granules become blue. When cool, store in a tight-fitting, covered container.

To restore it in the microwave, spread in an open cardboard box or microwavable dish and place on a rack in the middle of the oven. Set at medium high or high for about ten minutes. Interrupt to stir every few minutes. When blue and cool, store as described above.

MICROWAVE DRYING

Though the material must still be air dried to some extent, microwaving speeds up the process and helps to retain the color of flowers and grasses. Choose flowers that are partially opened. Petals fall off if the flower is in full bloom and buds do not

Dried Flowers

dry well. Leaves are dried separately because they dry faster than flowers. Most flowers hold their shape better if dried face-up. Branches with multiple blossoms should be dried lying flat. Let the dew dry on the petals and leaves before drying.

Insert toothpicks next to or through the stem of delicate flowers. The wire can be wrapped around the toothpick or poked through the flower head, hooked over a portion of the head, pulled back through and tightened after it's dried.

If petals are folded over one another, separate with toothpicks or pull them off with tweezers. Strip away the foliage and place the flowers on several sheets of paper towel in the microwave oven. Using a medium setting, microwave for about 2 1/2 minutes. Because of the variation in microwaves and the amount of moisture in plants it is impossible to give exact guidelines.

To prevent moisture forming and being re-absorbed by the flowers after they have been dried, replace the wet paper towels with dry ones, float a piece of saran over the flowers and allow them to remain in the microwave for 10-15 minutes with the door open. They will continue drying even after the oven is turned off. Hang flowers upside down for about three days. Wipe the microwave oven after each use.

Storing Dried Flowers and Plants

The safest way to store dried plants is in a long, shallow cardboard box. Poke holes in it so air can circulate and add small packets of desiccant to absorb moisture. Wrap bunches of like-flowers in tissue or newspaper and lay them in a head and foot arrangement. Don't overcrowd. Label box and store where the temperature is relatively constant.

Very delicate material can be stored hanging upside down with an umbrella of tissue paper to protect it from light and dust.

Ready for Use

Glycerine dried flowers can be misted with water and allowed to stand for 30 minutes to regain their suppleness.

Statice may be stored in the refrigerator for a few hours to regain suppleness.

Dried roses can be lightly steamed to expand the flower heads so you can fan out the leaves and petals. Filler material with small stems can be bundled into single units before being used in a design.

Just as fresh and silk flowers can be combined when making arrangements, silk and dried materials can also be used together. Adding baby's breath to an arrangement of silk flowers can have a softening effect, and dried star flowers or statice can add texture and color. Preserved eucalyptus, dried larkspur or dried bird of paradise leaves can be used as line flowers for a variety of color, texture and form in silk arrangements.

A Simple Dried Floral Arrangement

1. When making arrangements with dried flowers and leaves, fill container with oasis foam using blocks and chips to fill in empty places.

2. Add dried plants to establish over-all shape of arrangement.

3. Add medium size dried flora.

4. Highlight arrangement with flowers last so they don't get lost in all the dried material. In dried arrangements there is usually an abundance of material and focal flowers are spread throughout the design. Minimal arrangements with dried flowers have a tendency to look sparce and unfinished.

The dried arrangement can be something you keep transforming by adding new beautiful touches, changing the container, or trimming the length of the stems.

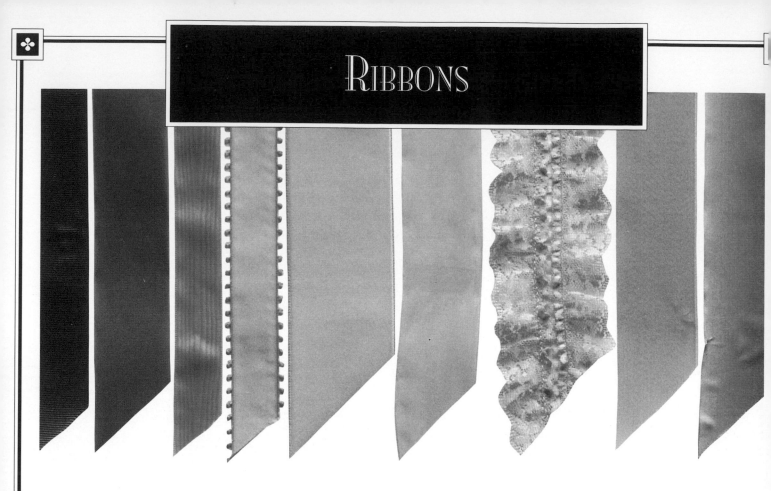

R ibbons create a feeling of elegant opulence and fanciful flights by softening angular shapes, gathering soft folds, nestling in small places and making sweeping gestures of texture and color. Some of the artful things to make with ribbons are very simple to create while others offer a little more challenge. With a little practice you can master them all.

Cotton– Casual, comfortable cotton is cut from bolt fabric and sized to maintain it's shape. Prints are usually one-sided; many stripes and plaids are considered two-sided, because they are woven. The ribbons found in craft stores are called cut-edge cotton. They can be cut lengthwise for narrower widths. Pleated cotton ribbons make interesting bows. Cottons are the most popular craft ribbons because they come in many beautiful patterns and colors.

Velvet–Elegant, rich velvet ribbons are made of a flock material. The colors and printed or embossed designs evoke images of celebrations and festivals. Velvet has a matte finish and is water resistant.

Satin–The most fluid of all ribbons, soft satins come in both cut-edge and woven-edge styles.

Cut-edge satin is less expensive, but it ravels along the lengthwise edges. Woven-edge satin ravels on the ends but not the sides. Woven-edge ribbons are usually washable but may shrink. They are water resistant.

Taffeta–Crisp, shiny, water-marked ribbons, very finely woven from silk or rayon have a cut edge. They make shapely, full-of-energy bows that hold their shape til you are ready for new ones.

Moire– Moire ribbon has a shimmering watermark finish. Stiff and substantial, it is well suited for making bows.

Burlap– Coarsely woven and heavily stiffened burlap can be made into bows that are subtle textured accents. Made of jute fibre, they lend a sturdy, comfortable, country feeling to a project.

Grosgrain and Faille–Richly-hued grosgrain and faille ribbons are made of woven blends and polyesters. Heavier than taffeta, they have delicate crosswise ribs-wider in grosgrain than in faille-creating a very subtle elasticity. Often used for trimming apparel, they both make shapely, lazy bows.

Lace–Floppy, lace bows have a mood of their own. They have finished edges and patterns that are often floral. Some ribbons have repeated perforations. Narrow ribbons can be threaded through to add extra sweetness or a color effect.

Piquot-edged–Piquot or feather edging is delicately looped threadwork. It appears on all types of ribbons and comes in prints or solid colors with lace edging or small trim on both sides.

French Wire Ribbon–Patterned and plain, opaque and silky sheer ribbons with tiny wire along the edges gives a new dimension to bows. Delicate bows hold their shape and heavier fabrics can be sculpted into dramatic designs.

Organdy– Gossamer, organdy ribbons can be either floppy or crisp. Some have beautiful silk-pattern trims.

Black and White– Ribbons take on graphic dimensions in black and white.They come in natural and polyester fabrics.

Outdoor Ribbon–Weatherproof ribbons are either plastic coated or made out of plastic material. They are perfect for porch centerpieces, hanging baskets, door decorations, and wreaths. Look for labels that recommend 'for outdoor use'.

SUGGESTIONS:

- Check manufacturer's directions before washing and allow for possible shrinkage.

- Use 24 gauge wire to secure center of bow. Twist as tightly as you can to make fluffy loops.

- Make larger loops and simpler bows when using coarse ribbons.

- Select fabrics and colors you are comfortable living with. When in doubt, choose natural.

- A glue gun can be very helpful when you don't seem to have enough fingers to hold ribbons and loops in place when making bows.

STREAMERS

They can link bows, plates, pictures etc. together or enhance and balance a bow; they can be draped in a pattern, looped or decorated and hung down a narrow wall. Streamers are the symbol of celebrations.

To attach streamers to a bow, cut a length of ribbon proportioned to fit bow and long enough for both streamers. Hold the two cut ends together and angle cut as desired. Attach center of streamers to center of bow with floral wire on the back.

TWISTERS

Twisters are a way to add a bouncy, splash of color to a plant or a present. Acetate or taffeta ribbons make the best twisters.

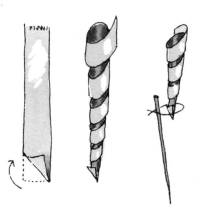

1. Cut a 10" piece of #9 ribbon. Fold one end up as shown in the illustration. Hold one end in your left hand while twisting the other end tightly with your right hand. The ribbon will form a spiral shape.

2. Wrap the ribbon ends with wire or floral tape and attach to wooden floral picks.

3. Cover the wooden picks with floral tape.

LOOPS

The symmetry and precision of bows are impressive, but loops combined with streamers provide a decorative style of their own. They can be made out of anything from silk to raffia, and once you know the basics you can embellish to suit the project or occasion.

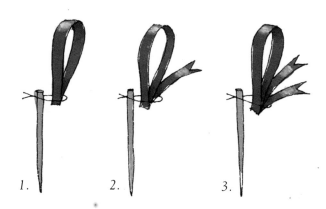

1.   2.   3.

1. To form a plain loop, use size #5 or #9 ribbon. Cut ribbon piece about 5" long. Bringing cut ends together, fold with right side of ribbon out. Gather ends around wooden floral pick and secure with wire.

2. To form a loop with a tail use extra ribbon. Cut end of streamer with one of the cut options.

3. To make a loop with two tails, cut a length of ribbon 10" long. Starting at the middle of the ribbon, fold in half with wrong sides together. Fold each side of doubled ribbons over again forming two tails. Pinch ribbon together at these last folds and secure with wire to wooden floral pick. Trim ends as desired.

Single Loop Bow

The single loop bow can be used for centerpieces, wreaths, tree boughs, dress collars, hats, sashes, live plants, napkin rings etc. It is the easiest bow to make if many are needed.

You can vary the basic single loop bow by adding extra tails, staggering the length of the tails, or exaggerating the diameter.

1. Cross ribbon ends making 4" tails. Where the ribbons cross is the center of the bow.

2. Bring the center together with the crossed ribbons. Pinch ribbons together and secure with a small piece of florist wire.

3. Cut tails at an angle or in points to finish.

4. Add decorative detail to center with glue gun or wire.

Florist Bow

1. Hold the ribbon right side up between thumb and index finger. Pinch the ribbon 4" from end and form a loop as large as you need, rolling the ribbon up and away from you. Place the long end of the ribbon between thumb and index finger to create the bow's center.

2. Make a half twist to the left so ribbon will be right side out and make bottom loop by rolling the ribbon down and away from you. Pinch the ribbon together at the bow center.

3. Continue making loops keeping loop sizes the same.

4. Before securing bow with wire, add button loop to top by twisting the end of the tail on top of the bow, (making sure the right side is out) over and under your thumb. Place wire through the small center loop, taking care to secure the end, and twist.

5. Arrange loops to form bow.

6. Cut desired length of ribbon to create a tie for the bow and place tie through the small center loop and knot in back.

Size Guide for Single Loop Bow		
Ribbon Size	Diameter of Bow with 4" tails	Yardage required
5	6"	5/8 yd.
9	7"	3/4 yd.
40	9"	1 yd.

Bows

All-purpose Bow

Shoelaces were probably the first bow you ever learned to make. Once that was mastered all kinds of opportunities opened up for you to try out your new skill: packages, dresses, ponytails...the list goes on. Here is how to make the perfect, all-purpose bow.

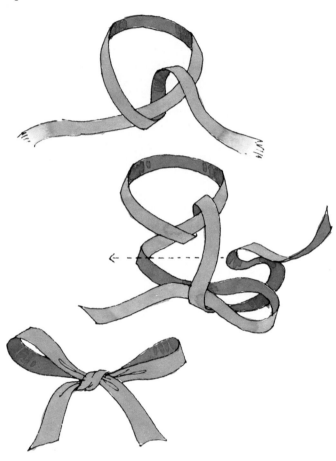

1. Starting with both ends even, cross the right ribbon underneath the left and make a half knot.

2. Keeping wrong sides of the ribbon together, make a loop between the thumb and index finger of the left hand.

3. Cross over the top of the loop with the ribbon right side up.

4. Finish second loop by pulling it up through the center space you've just created and pull tightly.

Fluffy Bow

An average size fluffy bow can be made with about 3 1/2 yds. of ribbon. The fluffy bow is a traditional gift wrap bow.

1. Wrap all the ribbon around fingers of right hand.

2. Hold the wrapped ribbon together at the center with one hand and cut two notches as shown.

3. Tie the center tightly with a short piece of ribbon or a twist of wire.

4. Spread the loops into a fluffy round bow.

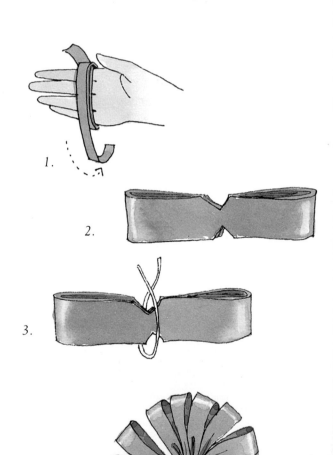

THREE-LOOP CRISSCROSS BOW

A regal looking bow that makes up nicely in double-faced satin looks great mounted on a wall over a picture (as shown) or any 'important looking' place. You will need three lengths of ribbon: one twenty-five inch and one fifty-inch length of 4 5/8" wide ribbon and a ten inch length of 1 1/2" wide ribbon. Note: For a contrasting edge, bind wider ribbon with different color, narrow ribbon after measuring.

1. Lay shorter piece of wide ribbon flat. Bring ends into center overlapping slightly.

2. Pleat at center and bind with florist's wire. Find center of longer piece, form a loop and bind with wire.

3. Iron a narrow ribbon in half lengthwise and place a short bow across the top of the long one below the loop.

4. Crisscross a narrow ribbon around the bow center.

5. Pull tightly to bind and stitch at back. Trim the ends evenly.

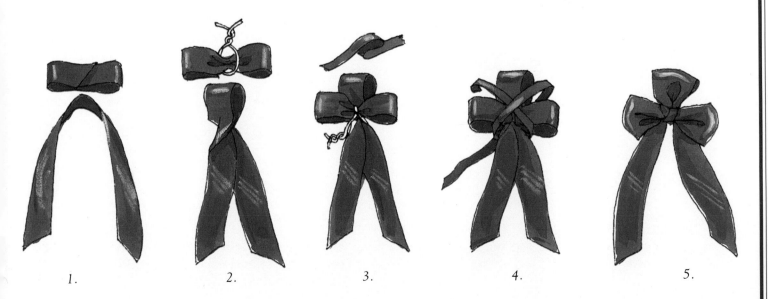

1.   2.   3.   4.   5.

Ribbon Rosettes

A bouquet of satin rosettes wired together and stitched to a wide ribbon gently gathers a gossamer curtain or the corners of a flower-filled canopy adding a feeling of gentleness and caring to special places in your home. Supple, satin ribbon works best for making rosettes which can also be sewn onto hats and dresses or hot glued on top of packages. When making a mature blossom, start with seven feet of 2 1/2" wide ribbon. (A bud requires four feet of 1" wide ribbon.)

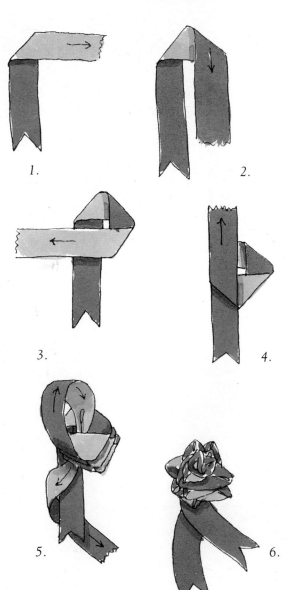

1. Lay ribbon on a flat surface and fold over at a ninety degree angle leaving five inches free at end.

2. Make another ninety degree fold working in a clockwise direction.

3. Repeat. Ribbon will form a square.

4. Continue folding ribbon clockwise on itself in a square pattern until you have built up four complete layers.

5. Slide pile onto one hand and push loose ribbon end down through center hole with other hand.

6. With free hand, twist the loose ribbon clockwise from below to make the folded ribbon squares start forming petals.

7. Bind tightly below petals with florist wire. Trim loose ends.

Storing Your Ribbons

The accomplished bow maker, like any artist, will find many opportunities to practice her or his skill. Eventually the question of where and how to keep the growing number of beautiful ribbons organized is bound to come up. A good way to keep them safe, orderly, and readily available is to hang them on a wall in a dry place away from sunlight. They tend to fade. Their decorative appearance will be both pleasing and inspiring.

- Expandable hat racks (verticle or horizontal)

- Coat racks (verticle or horizontal)

- Paper towel holders

- Towel holders

- Wooden drapery rods

- Rain gutters (Have a lumberyard cut a half-round gutter and cap the ends. Punch holes along the top edge and mount.)